This book is to be returned on or before
the last date stamped below.

Energy foods

Energy foods

Nic Rowley and Kirsten Hartvig

DUNCAN BAIRD PUBLISHERS

LONDON

Energy foods is dedicated with love to Lilly Marie Jensen

Energy foods
Nic Rowley and Kirsten Hartvig

First published in the United Kingdom and Ireland in 2000 by
Duncan Baird Publishers Ltd
Sixth Floor, Castle House
75–76 Wells Street
London W1P 3RE

Conceived, created and designed by Duncan Baird Publishers

Managing Editor: Judy Dean
Editor: Ingrid Court-Jones
Designer: Steve Painter, with Rachel Goldsmith
Commissioned photography: Sian Irvine
Home Economist and Food Stylist: Pippin Britz

British Library Cataloguing-in-Publication Data:
A catalogue record for this book is available from the British Library

10 9 8 7 6 5 4 3 2 1

ISBN: 1-900131-83-8

Typeset in Rotis Sans Serif and Univers
Colour reproduction by Colourscan, Singapore
Printed by Imago, Singapore

Contents

Introduction

This book is about maximizing the nutritional value of everything we eat so that we can get the most out of life. *Energy Foods* is written in the belief that healthy food should be tasty and colourful, with exciting flavours and interesting textures, and in the knowledge that anyone can increase their vitality by improving the quality of their diet.

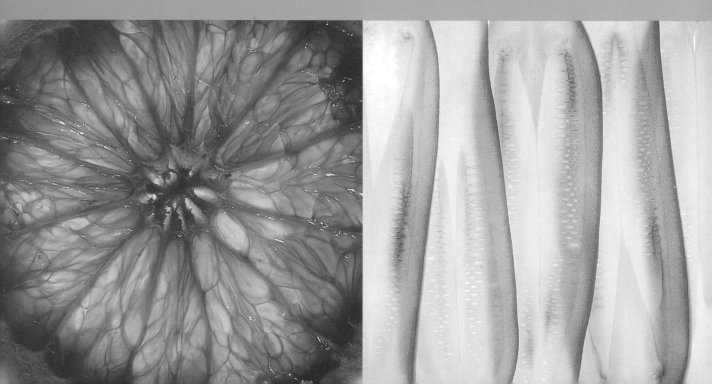

Rather than entering into long explanations with complex charts, we have distilled up-to-date nutritional knowledge and blended it with proven naturopathic wisdom to help you create a new and exciting way to eat, packed with life and power. All the breakfast, lunch, dinner and snack recipes put energy food principles into practice, each one rated for its Energy Boost, and listing its main Nutrients and Body Benefits. We hope that you will enjoy reading and, above all, using this book – and that it will inspire you to make *Energy Foods* part of your daily life.

ABOUT THE RECIPE RATING SYSTEM
All the recipes in *Energy Foods* are packed with natural energy. For quick reference, each recipe is given a star rating (maximum five stars) to make the energy benefits of any one dish immediately apparent.

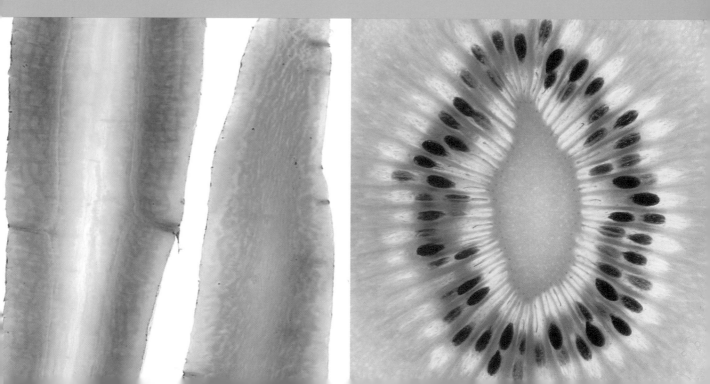

chapter one

The natural way

If we want our bodies to be healthy, and to function at peak performance level, the best long-term investment we can make is to eat the natural way.

By adopting a mainly plant-centred diet including fresh fruit, raw vegetables, pulses and whole grains, supplemented by organically reared meat and fish if we wish, we can provide ourselves with all the basic nutrients we need to increase our energy levels and live life to the full. Another benefit of healthy eating is that it can also stimulate our often forgotten, in-built capacity to heal ourselves.

Natural health awareness

nutrition for vitality

In a world of rich diversity there is one thing on which scientists, scholars and sages all agree – life is the movement of energy. From first heartbeat to last breath, our bodies are constantly transforming food-energy into warmth, movement, thought, emotion and activity. By eating in tune with nature and tapping into the vitality of fresh, organic ingredients, we can move closer to the sources of life-energy – the sun and the soil – and so enhance our health and wellbeing. Here are five natural nutritional principles to help you transform your diet into one based on energy foods.

Eat fresh

Too much refined and processed food robs the body of vital nutrients and increases our intake of fat, sugar and additives.

Eat organic

Food that is free from chemical residues and genetic manipulation improves our health and that of the planet.

Eat raw

Eating fresh fruit and raw salad each day increases our fibre and reduces our salt intake, helps to optimize our absorption of protein and ensures a rich supply of cancer-busting phytochemicals (health-enhancing substances found only in plant foods).

Eat plants

Invest in your long-term health by including more plant-based food in your diet. Try to eat more vegetables and less meat. Replace cow's milk by soya, rice, oat or almond milk, and replace butter with unhydrogenated plant spreads, free from trans-fatty acids. Use polyunsaturated plant oils (such as safflower or sunflower oil) in cooking and salad dressings.

Eat smart

Eat when you are hungry, stop when you are satisfied. Chew your food well and try not to eat when you are angry, frustrated, stressed or in a hurry. Cut down on refined sugar – use honey, and maple and fruit syrups in place of sugar whenever you can. Also decrease your intake of stimulants – beverages containing caffeine give you short-term energy at the expense of long-term vitality.

Body power

As societies have become more urbanized and developed, so the number of people suffering from the effects of heart disease, strokes and cancer has increased. At the root of these changing health patterns is the move away from a diet based on grains, fruits and vegetables to one based on processed foods, fat, sugar and animal produce.

The scientific evidence is clear: if we want to have healthy bodies, we should change our food focus and put fresh fruit, fresh vegetables, pulses and whole grains back in the centre of our plates (supplemented by fresh, organically reared meat and fish according to taste). Here are some of the most important components of a healthy, energy-full diet.

Calcium

Crucial for building and maintaining healthy bones and teeth, calcium also plays an important role in the function of nerves, muscles, enzymes and hormones. Most plant foods contain calcium – spinach, watercress, parsley, dried figs, nuts, seeds, molasses, seaweed and soya are all rich suppliers. Gram for gram, bean curd (tofu) contains four times more calcium than whole cow's milk.

Proteins

The building blocks of the body, proteins consist of long, folded chains of amino acids. It is not widely known that plant foods contain protein and that vegetables, grains and pulses are all good sources – gram for gram, soya flour contains more protein than beef steak, and butterbeans have more than plaice.

Complex carbohydrates

Complex carbohydrates are made of sugar molecules linked together into long, branched chains. Found only in foods made from plants, they are a major source of energy in our diet and have beneficial effects on the way we absorb and use other nutrients. Foods containing complex carbohydrates, such as bread and pasta, are usually rich in vitamins, minerals and trace elements.

Antioxidants

In the process of metabolism, our body's cells produce molecules called free radicals, which can attack and harm cell membranes. Antioxidants, such as beta-carotene, vitamin C, vitamin E and selenium, neutralize these unstable chemicals, in turn protecting our cells. Fruit, vegetables, nuts, grains and cold-pressed plant oils are the main sources of antioxidants in our diet.

Essential fatty acids

Two polyunsaturated fatty acids, linoleic acid and alpha-linolenic acid, are known as essential fatty acids because they can be obtained only from the food we eat. They are necessary for normal growth of the fetus during pregnancy, and play a central role in blood-clotting and healing wounds. They also help to maintain the health of the brain and the cells of other parts of our bodies. Important sources of essential fatty acids include green leaves (such as lettuce and cabbage) and vegetable oils (for example, sunflower, safflower, wheatgerm and corn oils).

Brain power

energy foods for healthy minds

Energy foods benefit the brain as well as the body. They provide glucose and micronutrients, such as thiamine, riboflavin, niacin, vitamin C and iron, to maximize our mental performance and to help us cope better under pressure. They enhance the carbohydrate–protein balance in our diet to make us calmer and more alert, and improve the quality of our sleep. They also reduce our reaction to common causes of food intolerance and make us less prone to depression, headaches and general tiredness. Here are six simple ways to boost your brain power.

Kick-start vitality

Eat a good breakfast to avoid low blood sugar in the late morning, and to sharpen your memory and mental clarity. (See pp.38–41 for a selection of delicious high-energy breakfasts to launch the day.)

Snack often

Boost your vitality mid-morning and mid-afternoon with a quick-fix snack or drink (pp.66–71). These will help to keep you alert right up until the end of the day.

Eat regularly

Keep regular meal times and do not skip meals. Research shows that eating several small meals per day helps the brain to work more efficiently than having one or two big meals.

Oil the cogs

Ensure your body gets a rich supply of essential fatty acids by including salads, green, leafy vegetables and some safflower and sunflower oil in your diet. Low in saturated animal fats, energy foods are high in plant polyunsaturates, which keep our brain cells in peak condition.

Power sleep

Take a power nap after your midday meal. Brain efficiency naturally drops after lunch, and the short time it takes to recharge your batteries will more than repay itself in extra mental energy later in the day.

Pump iron

Eat more wholegrain cereals, pulses and green vegetables to boost your iron intake. Drink a glass of vitamin C-rich, fresh fruit juice each day to maximize iron absorption.

Nature's best
fresh, seasonal and organic

To build a durable house, you need good foundations. To build a strong and healthy body, you need good food. As everything we eat is either a plant or comes from an animal that eats plants, it follows that the foundation of good food is healthy plants. And every gardener knows that healthy plants grow in healthy soil. So, if we really care about our food and health, our first concern should be for the health of the land.

The problem is that most people simply regard food as something bought in the grocery store or supermarket. Though we may feel uncomfortable about antibiotic, hormone and pesticide residues, diseased cattle, food irradiation, genetically modified crops and the hundred-and-one other "food safety scares" that seem to be part of modern living, our relationship with the farmer and the land is now so distant that we often feel powerless to create change. But once we remember that food production and supply systems depend on consumer demand, it becomes clear that we *can* make a difference by choosing carefully which produce we buy.

Organic fruit and vegetables, which have been grown using traditional, pesticide-free methods with natural fertilizers, contain more nutrients and also often taste better than mass-market produce. So every time we eat organic, locally or regionally grown, fresh, seasonal, minimally processed and minimally packaged energy foods, we put back one more brick in the pyramid of health. Next time you shop at the supermarket, bear in mind that by "going organic" you are setting in motion a knock-on effect that will produce healthier soil, healthier plants, healthier animals and, ultimately, healthier people.

24-hour detox

Detoxing will make you feel lighter in yourself, and help to reduce your susceptibility to stress and illness. But the most immediate and striking improvement you will notice after detoxifying is that you will have much more energy. Other benefits include shinier hair, clearer skin, better sleep, improved digestion, sweeter breath, a more sensitive sense of smell, a clearer brain and a calmer state of mind.

Detoxification involves using all available resources for body healing and regeneration. Every now and then, use the following, simple, 24-hour plan to give your digestive system a rest and to help your body to rid itself of accumulated toxins. Choose a day when you can be sure of peace and quiet, and have a comfortable, warm environment in which you can sleep as much as you wish.

The day before starting your detox, cut out all stimulants (tea, coffee, chocolate, tobacco, alcohol and so on); sugar (sweets, cakes, fizzy drinks); meat and dairy products; and processed foods.

On the day, follow the menu plan as shown opposite. Take as much rest as you can, keep warm and drink pure water, little and often. Spend some time outside in the fresh air, but keep any activities gentle.

After your 24-hour detox, stay off stimulants and do not eat processed foods for a week. Take stock of your diet and listen to your body – it knows instinctively which foods are good for you and which are not.

Detox menu plan

Breakfast
Fresh fruit salad (see p. 41)

Mid-morning
1 cup nettle tea

Lunch
$1/4$ melon, followed by fruit
salad comprising:
1 thick slice pineapple, chunked
1 sliced banana
1 apple, cored and chopped
1 pear, cored and chopped
6 grapes, halved and pipped
5 tablespoons unsweetened fruit juice

Mid-afternoon
1 cup thyme tea

Dinner
$1/2$ papaya
1 mango

After dinner
1 cup camomile tea

Note: We do not recommend that you do
the 24-hour detox during menstruation, nor
if you are pregnant or breast feeding. If you
are taking medication, check with your
doctor before following the plan.

chapter two

Foods
for life

Energy foods are the foundations of health
and vitality. They fall into natural groups
which supply the different nutrients we
need to provide an energy-rich diet.

As the level of energy that we need on a daily basis varies depending

on our activity, our age, and the type of metabolism we have, it makes

sense to base our diet on those foods which optimize our energy

output accordingly – fresh fruit and vegetables, pulses, pasta and

wholemeal bread. In the following pages we take a look at the most

important food groups and learn how to get the best out of them.

Fruit and vegetables

nature's own convenience foods

Fruit and vegetables are our link to the vital energies of the sun and the earth. The plants that bear them use sunlight to make the starches which are our primary source of complex carbohydrates, and an important supplier of energy to our bodies. And fresh fruit and vegetables are full of proteins, oils and minerals, which help us to share in the goodness in the soil. When our diet is rich in such foods, we fulfil our nutritional needs without having to take supplements.

Nature's own energy foods, fruit and vegetables are delicious, relatively inexpensive and can be enjoyed raw or cooked at any time, with a minimum of preparation.

Here are some good reasons to include fresh fruit and vegetables in your diet.

✪ Fruit and vegetables are naturally high in fibre and low in cholesterol, as well as being rich in polyunsaturates, and essential amino and fatty acids. They contain no harmful saturated fats or trans-fatty acids.

✪ It is now proven beyond doubt that eating more fruit and vegetables protects our bodies against most cancers.

✪ Eating natural fruit and vegetable fibre reduces the chances of suffering from heart problems and bowel disease.

✪ Fruit and vegetables contain a cocktail of health-enhancing phytochemicals, which play a crucial role in our metabolism and boost our immune system.

✪ Eating at least five portions of fruit and vegetables daily can help us to shrug off minor ailments.

Raw energy

eating it like it is

Human beings are the only creatures who do not eat most of their food fresh and raw. Although cooking reduces the amount of time we spend eating – cooked food requires less chewing – it alters the chemical make-up of food and can destroy essential nutrients. Vitamins A, C and E (important antioxidants), thiamin and folic acid are damaged or destroyed by heat. The structure of amino acids, such as lysine, can also be changed by the cooking process, with the result that they cannot be absorbed by our bodies.

Eating some raw food every day offers many health benefits. It helps us maintain a natural water balance, reduces our salt intake, and ensures that we obtain the maximum benefit from the large variety of cancer-protective phytochemicals contained in fresh fruit and vegetables. Raw food diets can improve our resistance to minor illnesses such as colds and 'flu, and also help us deal more effectively with chronic conditions such as arthritis and diabetes.

As it is not always practical or convenient to eat raw food, here are some tips to help minimize vitamin and mineral loss when cooking fresh, organic vegetables.

✪ When cleaning vegetables, keep washing to the minimum that is consistent with good hygiene.

✪ Do not pre-soak vegetables, or start cooking them in cold water. Put them straight into boiling water or steam them.

✪ Cook vegetables as lightly as possible – they should be firm and tender, not soggy.

✪ Make sauces and gravies with the vegetable cooking-water so that you can benefit from any vitamins and minerals that they have lost to the water.

✪ Try shallow-frying chopped vegetables in a little oil, then cooking them in a covered pan with a little water – a great way to preserve both flavour and nutrients.

Cereal grains

stamina foods that go the distance

The main source of energy and protein for people in the world today is cereal grains. Here is a guide to the most important varieties.

Rice has been a staple food in the East for more than 5,000 years. De-hulled but unpolished, it is a great source of protein, energy, fibre and B-vitamins. "Wild rice" is a native American grain, unrelated to common rice, but also highly nutritious.

Oats are a high-protein cereal, rich in iron and soluble fibre. By lowering the body's blood cholesterol levels they reduce the risk of coronary heart disease. Naturopaths value oats' ability to ease stress and soothe tired nerves. Uniquely, they lose little of their nutritional value when commercially processed into flakes or oatmeal.

Maize (also known as corn) originated in the Americas and was brought to Europe by the explorer Christopher Columbus (1451–1506). It has a particular claim to be called an "energy food" as it yields a large energy-rich crop in a small area of land. Dishes combining maize, beans and green vegetables are especially nutritious.

Buckwheat was first grown in China but is now popular in central and Eastern Europe. Its traditional reputation for being "warming and drying" makes it a good source of energy in winter. Kasha, made from buckwheat groats roasted briefly in a dry pan then cooked in vegetable stock with a bayleaf until soft, makes a nourishing and tasty alternative to rice.

Quinoa and amaranth are ancient Andean plants that thrive in mountain climates. Among the most nutritious of all grains and rich in protein and minerals, they can be used to add variety to savoury casseroles, breakfast cereals and biscuits.

Millet is a staple in many parts of Africa, China and India, and the dietary cornerstone of the healthy and long-lived Hunza people of north-west Pakistan. Now neglected in the West, it makes a delicious alternative to oats in porridge, and is a good source of magnesium and iron.

Rye was the main bread-making ingredient in medieval Northern Europe, and enjoys a long-standing "muscle-making" reputation in Scandinavia, Germany and Eastern Europe. Traditional "sour-dough" rye bread can turn a simple sandwich into a nutritious meal, and rye crispbreads are a source of protein as well as energy.

Wheat is the world's most popular grain, accounting for more than 25 per cent of global cereal production. A very versatile foodstuff, it is used to make bread, pasta, couscous and tabouleh.

Peas, beans and lentils

energy boosters in small packages

Peas, beans and lentils (also known as pulses or legumes) have a history stretching back at least 7,000 years, and were known to civilizations from ancient Egypt to Mexico. They are packed with top-quality protein, complex carbohydrates, fibre, vitamins and minerals so they are extremely satisfying yet have a negligible fat content. Their ability to lower blood cholesterol helps to prevent heart disease, and the slow way in which they are digested and absorbed makes them an ideal food for diabetics. Peas, beans and lentils are inexpensive, versatile and easy to store.

Here are some ways to make the most of these natural energy boosters.

✪ When buying dried pulses, look for a rich colour and regular shape. Choose a reliable organic supplier and avoid old stock.

✪ Pulses should be cooked until they are soft and tender. Add a small potato to the cooking water of dried pulses that require pre-soaking – it makes them easier to digest. Do not add salt until just before serving.

✪ Help your digestive system to adapt to eating pulses. Start off with split peas, dhals and lentils, or try some bottled (pre-cooked) organic, lima beans or chick peas.

✪ Pulses are highly concentrated, high-protein foods best enjoyed in moderation. 1–3 oz (30–75 g) dry weight per day is ample.

✪ Soya bean, mung bean and chick pea sprouts are delicious additions to salads, adding vital nutrients as well as flavour.

Pasta
ideal fuel for action

The earliest surviving written reference to pasta dates from the thirteenth century, but depictions have been found in Etruscan murals dating from as early as c.400BC. Today the peoples of Italy and northern China eat pasta as a staple food, while all over the world it has become a popular meal for anyone wanting a quick-cooking and nutritious source of energy.

Durum wheat – the traditional basis of Italian pasta – is particularly high in the protein gluten, which makes it easy to form into the many shapes beloved of pasta connoisseurs: spaghetti, lasagne, penne, macaroni and fettucine, to name but a few. The density of durum wheat means that it is digested more slowly than other wheat products, releasing a steady flow of energy into the body.

Here are some variations on the pasta theme which you can use to add new flavours and textures to your meals.

✪ Powdered beetroot, spinach, tomatoes, carrots and herbs can be mixed with durum wheat flour to enhance the visual and nutritional quality of pasta, as well as the taste.

✪ Wholemeal pasta – durum wheat flour mixed with other wheat flours – is richer in vitamins and heavier in texture than other pasta. It has a distinctive, "nutty" flavour which is sometimes considered an acquired taste.

✪ Noodles enriched with amaranth or quinoa (see p.29) are highly nutritious, and lesser-known pastas such as *udon* (Japanese rice and wheat spaghetti) and *soba* (made with buckwheat, wheat and herbs) make an exotic change.

Breads

A symbol of life and abundance, bread has been at the heart of human nutrition for more than 15,000 years. It is eaten around the world in a multitude of forms ranging from baguettes to bagels, pumpernickel to soda bread, chapatis to tortillas. It is a vital supplier of energy, protein, fibre, B-vitamins, iron, calcium and trace elements. Bread can be made from any cereal, but the flour of wheat is particularly suitable as it contains gluten, a protein that becomes sticky when mixed with water. The gluten traps the gas produced by fermenting yeast inside the dough and makes the bread rise.

To say that home-made, wholemeal bread is healthiest is almost a cliché, but here are some facts that show it is based on truth.

✪ White flours are "enriched" with vitamins and minerals, but enriching does not replace the vitamin B6, vitamin E, folic acid, pantothenic acid, magnesium and zinc lost during the refining process.

✪ Commercially produced "added bran" flours are less digestible than traditional stoneground and sifted flours in which the non-nutritious, outer covering of the wheat grain, known as the "bee's wing", has been removed.

✪ To cut costs and production times, industrial bread manufacturers use a process involving chemicals and mechanical mixers, instead of traditional kneading and proving.

✪ White loaves typically contain only half the fibre of their wholemeal counterparts.

✪ Bread consumption in industrialized countries has decreased by half in the past hundred years. During the same period, heart disease, cancer, and bowel problems have shown a dramatic increase. Eating wholemeal bread helps safeguard long-term health and adds flavour and substance to any diet.

chapter three

Energy recipes

This section presents delicious, high-energy recipes from around the world, with many drawn from the particularly healthy diets of the East and the Mediterranean regions.

The recipes are designed to provide your body with all the nutrition

it needs throughout the day. Beginning with high-energy breakfasts,

there are also power-packed lunches and energy-sustaining dinners,

as well as simple snacks and drinks which will give you a boost at any

time. Now you can eat healthily all day.

zesty**break**fasts

launching the day

Muesli with fruit and nuts

Makes 1 serving

1 portion sugar-free muesli base (a mixture
of oat, wheat, barley, rice and rye)
2 tablespoons chopped nuts mixed with
seeds (e.g. walnuts, hazelnuts, almonds,
sunflower seeds)
2 dates, chopped
2 dried apricots, chopped
1 tablespoon dessicated coconut
5 tablespoons seasonal fresh fruit
or berries, chopped
Soya, almond, rice or oat milk to taste

1. Mix the muesli base with the nuts, seeds,
dried fruit and coconut.
2. Sprinkle the fresh fruit or berries on top.
3. Serve with your chosen milk to taste, and
a glass of freshly squeezed grapefruit or
orange juice.

Energy Boost:	✪ ✪ ✪ ✪ ✪
Nutrients:	Vitamins A, C, & E, B-group; calcium, magnesium, iron, zinc, selenium; essential fatty acids
Body Benefits:	Immune and digestive systems

Belgian porridge

Makes 1 serving

3–4 tablespoons rolled oats
1 tablespoon chopped nuts mixed with seeds
(e.g. walnuts, hazelnuts, almonds, and
sunflower seeds)
1 tablespoon dried fruit (e.g. raisins or
apricots)
Water
Pinch of sea salt
Soya milk
1/2 apple, grated
Maple syrup (optional)

1. Put the oats in a saucepan with the nuts,
seeds and dried fruit.

2. Add twice the volume of water, a pinch
of sea salt and bring the mixture to the boil,
stirring continuously.
3. Simmer gently until the oats swell and
the porridge thickens, gradually adding a
little cold soya milk. Stir from time to time
to prevent the porridge sticking to the pan.
4. Serve topped with grated apple, maple
syrup and soya milk to taste.

Energy Boost:	✪ ✪ ✪ ✪
Nutrients:	Vitamins E, B-group; calcium, magnesium, iron; essential fatty acids
Body Benefits:	Digestive, circulatory and nervous systems; heart

Filled pancakes

Makes 12 pancakes

Pancake batter
8 oz / 225 g wheat flour
2 teaspoons baking powder
Pinch of sea salt
4 fl oz / 125 ml soya milk
5 fl oz / 150 ml water
3 tablespoons safflower oil
Grapeseed oil for cooking

1. Sift the flour and baking powder into a bowl, add salt and mix well.
2. Pour in the soya milk a little at a time, stirring continuously with a whisk.
3. Continue stirring and gradually mix in the water to form a thick batter.
4. Slowly pour in the oil and continue to stir until completely blended.
5. Allow the mixture to stand while you prepare the pancake filling.
6. Cook the pancakes one at a time in a frying pan in grapeseed oil.

Pancake filling
2 bananas, thinly sliced
2 peaches, thinly sliced
2 apricots, thinly sliced
12 strawberries, chopped
Cinnamon
3 tablespoons chopped almonds or pistachios, lightly roasted in a dry frying pan
Maple syrup to taste

1. Mix the bananas, peaches, apricots and strawberries in a bowl.
2. Place a couple of spoonfuls of the fruit mixture in the centre of each pancake, sprinkle with cinnamon and chopped nuts, top with maple syrup and roll up. Serve immediately.

Energy Boost:	✪ ✪ ✪ ✪
Nutrients:	Vitamins A, C & E; iron; essential fatty acids
Body Benefit:	Immune system

Fresh fruit salad

Makes 1 serving

$^1/_2$ papaya, deseeded and sliced

1 banana, sliced

1 pear (or 1 apple), cored and sliced

1 portion fresh soft fruits or berries
   (e.g. raspberries, strawberries,
   apricots, peaches, nectarines,
   plums, cherries)

5 grapes, halved

5 tablespoons unsweetened fruit juice

1 teaspoon maple syrup (optional)

Mix together all the fruits in a bowl,
then add the fruit juice and maple
syrup. Serve with a glass of freshly
squeezed grapefruit or orange juice.

Energy Boost:	✪ ✪ ✪
Nutrients:	Vitamins A & C; calcium, magnesium, zinc
Body Benefits:	Immune system; detoxifying

Penne pesto with Italian salad

Serves 4

Penne pesto
10 oz / 300 g penne or other pasta
5 tablespoons pine nuts
1 teaspoon coarse sea salt
3 tablespoons fresh basil, finely chopped
   (or 3 teaspoons dried)
4 tablespoons extra virgin olive oil
1-2 cloves garlic, crushed

1. Boil the pasta in salted water with a little olive oil (to stop it sticking together).
2. While the pasta is cooking, grind the pine nuts and sea salt in a mortar or blender.
3. Add the basil, olive oil and garlic to the ground pine nuts and salt, and mix well.
4. Transfer the pesto to a small bowl.
5. Put the cooked pasta in a separate dish. Serve the pesto and pasta with Italian salad.

Italian salad
1 small radicchio, shredded
1 cup fresh peas, shelled
1 carrot, finely diced
2 ripe tomatoes, diced
1 yellow pepper, diced
$^1/_2$ fennel, diced
$^1/_2$ red onion, diced
4 radishes, sliced
4 button mushrooms, thinly sliced
Fresh basil leaves to garnish

Put the shredded radicchio in a large salad bowl and add the rest of the ingredients in the order shown above. Garnish with basil and serve with walnut dressing.

Walnut dressing
Juice of $^1/_2$ a ripe lemon
Sea salt and black pepper
1 teaspoon soya sauce
2 teaspoons maple syrup
1 teaspoon Dijon mustard
$^1/_2$ teaspoon curry powder
1 teaspoon tahini
5 fl oz / 150 ml walnut oil
Extra virgin olive oil to taste

1. Put the lemon juice, salt, pepper, soya sauce, maple syrup, mustard and curry powder into a bowl and whisk with a fork.
2. Add the tahini and continue whisking until the consistency is smooth.
3. Gradually stir in the walnut oil.
4. Add olive oil to taste.

Energy Boost:	✪ ✪ ✪ ✪ ✪
Nutrients:	Vitamins A, C & E; niacin, thiamin, folate; calcium, magnesium, iron, manganese, zinc; essential fatty acids
Body Benefits:	Heart; circulatory system

Baba ganoush
with three-root salad

Serves 4

Baba ganoush
1 medium eggplant (aubergine)
1 clove garlic, crushed
3 tablespoons tahini
3 tablespoons lemon juice
Sea salt
Fresh parsley, finely chopped, to garnish

1. Prick the eggplant with a fork, then place under a moderate grill, turning frequently until the skin is charred and loosened from the flesh.
2. Cool the eggplant by holding it under running water for a minute, then cut in half lengthways and scrape out the flesh with a tablespoon.
3. Chop the flesh finely, put it in a bowl and mix with the garlic, tahini, lemon juice and salt.
4. Put in a serving bowl, garnish with parsley and serve.

Three-root salad
3-4 medium carrots, scrubbed
1 small beetroot, peeled
$\frac{1}{4}$ medium celeriac, peeled

Grate all the ingredients, mix together in a salad bowl and serve with pitta bread and baba ganoush.

Energy Boost:	✪ ✪ ✪
Nutrients:	Vitamins A, C, & E; folate; zinc, calcium, iron
Body Benefit:	Immune system

Tabouleh Orientale
with Korean cucumber

Serves 4

Tabouleh Orientale

7 oz / 200 g couscous (dry weight)
4 tablespoons safflower oil
1 green pepper, chopped into small cubes
2 tomatoes, chopped into small cubes
4 small scallions (spring onions), finely sliced
1 Iceberg lettuce, finely chopped
Fresh mint, finely chopped
Fresh parsley, finely chopped
4 tablespoons lemon juice
Sea salt; pepper to taste

1. Put 8 fl oz / 250 mls of water in a medium-sized saucepan, add 1 teaspoon salt, and bring to the boil.
2. Add the couscous and remove the pan immediately from the heat.
3. Stir once and allow the couscous to absorb all the water.
4. Add the safflower oil to the couscous and transfer to a salad bowl.
5. Add the rest of the ingredients to the couscous and mix together.

Korean cucumber

1 medium cucumber, finely sliced
1 medium onion, finely sliced
2 teaspoons sea salt
3 tablespoons lemon juice
Pinch of cayenne pepper
2 tablespoons tahini
1 tablespoon sesame oil
Gomasio to garnish

1. Put the cucumber and onion slices in a bowl.
2. Sprinkle over the salt and mix well.
3. Add the lemon juice, cayenne pepper, tahini and sesame oil.
4. Mix again, garnish with gomasio and serve with tabouleh Orientale.

Energy Boost:	✪ ✪ ✪
Nutrients:	Vitamins C & E; B-group; zinc, calcium, iron; essential fatty acids
Body Benefit:	Immune system

Amanida Catalana

Serves 4

1 Little Gem lettuce, shredded
$\frac{1}{2}$ yellow pepper, cut in long thin slices
$\frac{1}{2}$ red pepper, cut in long thin slices
2 tomatoes, cut in thin boats
2 tablespoons sweetcorn
1 red salad onion, finely sliced
2 tablespoons capers
2 tablespoons brazil nuts, finely chopped

1. Place the shredded lettuce on a flat salad plate and add the yellow and red peppers to form stripes on the lettuce.
2. Decorate with the tomatoes and sweetcorn.
3. Garnish with the onion, capers and brazil nuts. Serve with rice, and with walnut dressing (see p.42).

Energy Boost:	✪ ✪ ✪ ✪
Nutrients:	Vitamins A & C; B-group; selenium, iron, zinc, calcium, magnesium; essential fatty acids
Body Benefits:	Immune, circulatory, digestive and nervous systems

Soupe au pistou

3 tablespoons extra virgin olive oil
1 leek, sliced
2 onions, halved and sliced lengthways
2-3 cloves garlic, crushed
$\frac{1}{4}$ medium celeriac, diced
2 carrots, chopped
2 medium potatoes, diced
3 tomatoes, skinned and cut into thin boats
$3\frac{1}{2}$ oz / 100 g green beans, sliced
1 zucchini (courgette), chopped
3 pints / 1.5 litres vegetable stock or water
7 oz / 200 g cooked white haricot beans
3 tablespoons fresh basil (or 3 teaspoons dried) finely chopped
2 oz / 50 g small macaroni
Sea salt and pepper

1. Heat the oil in a large pan and soften (but do not brown) the leek, onions and garlic.
2. Add the celeriac, carrots and potatoes, stirring continously as they heat through, then put in the tomatoes.
3. Cook for 2 minutes. Add the green beans and zucchini.
4. Pour in the stock, bring to the boil, and simmer. Add the haricot beans and 2 tablespoons of fresh basil. Boil again.
5. Add the macaroni, salt and pepper. Simmer for a further 10-15 minutes. Add the rest of the basil, adjust seasoning and serve with thick slices of fresh country bread.

Energy Boost:	✪ ✪ ✪ ✪
Nutrients:	Viamins A, C & E; thiamin, niacin, folate; iron, zinc, magnesium, calcium, manganese
Body Benefits:	Heart; circulatory, nervous and urino-genital systems; skin

Gazpacho de Campo

Serves 4

1 cucumber, finely chopped
1 lb / 450 g tomatoes, skinned and
    finely chopped
1 onion, finely chopped
1 green pepper, finely chopped
2 cloves garlic, finely chopped
5 tablespoons extra virgin olive oil
3 tablespoons lemon juice
3 tablespoons raspberry vinegar
Sea salt and pepper
1 small bunch fresh dill, finely chopped
Croutons and ice cubes

1. Set aside a quarter of each of the chopped
vegetables, except the garlic, and blend the
rest with the olive oil, lemon juice and
vinegar to a thick, smooth consistency.
2. Season to taste, transfer to a soup tureen,
and chill for at least an hour.
3. Garnish with dill and serve with rest of
finely chopped vegetables, croutons and ice
cubes in separate side dishes.

Energy Boost:	✪ ✪ ✪
Nutrients:	Vitamins A and E; niacin, vitamin B6; iron, zinc; essential fatty acids
Body Benefits:	Immune, circulatory and urino-genital systems; skin

Crunchy Spanish salad
with hot sesame sauce

Serves 4

Crunchy Spanish salad

1 small Iceberg lettuce, finely shredded

1 small green pepper, finely chopped

2 sticks celery, finely chopped

1 carrot, grated

1 handful grapes, halved and pipped

1 handful bean sprouts

Put the lettuce in a large bowl with the pepper, celery and carrot. Garnish with the grapes and bean sprouts.

Hot sesame sauce

3 tablespoons tahini

3 tablespoons water

3 tablespoons lemon juice

1 clove garlic, crushed

1 teaspoon fresh ginger, grated

Pinch of cayenne pepper

$^1/_4$ teaspoon sea salt

Mix all the ingredients well and heat gently in a saucepan. Serve with crunchy Spanish salad and thick slices of crusty bread.

Energy Boost:	✪ ✪ ✪
Nutrients:	Vitamins A & E; folate; zinc
Body Benefit:	Immune system

Alligator sandwiches
with red coleslaw

Makes 4 sandwiches

Alligator sandwich filling
2 avocados, peeled, stoned and sliced
4 Iceberg lettuce leaves
4 slices of tomato
4 tablespoons alfalfa sprouts
4 scallions (spring onions) thinly sliced

Alligator dressing
4 tablespoons lemon juice
2 teaspoons French mustard
1 clove garlic, crushed
2 teaspoons tomato paste
12 black olives, stoned and finely chopped
1 tablespoon fresh parsley, finely chopped
5–10 drops Tabasco sauce to taste
Extra virgin olive oil to taste
Sea salt and pepper to taste

1. Prepare the filling ingredients and
set aside.
2. Mix dressing ingredients together into a
coarse paste.
3. Halve and toast 4 large, wholemeal,
sesame rolls.
4. Coat the insides of the rolls with dressing
and fill with equal portions of salad mixture.

Red coleslaw
2 medium beetroots, grated
4 eating apples, grated
Juice of $^1/_2$ lemon, squeezed
2 tablespoons safflower oil
1 teaspoon fresh, grated horseradish
   (or a small, finely chopped, shallot)
$^1/_2$ teaspoon cinnamon
Zest of 1 orange

1. Put the beetroot and apple in a bowl.
2. Add the lemon juice, safflower oil,
horseradish and cinnamon, and mix well.
3. Garnish with orange zest and serve with
alligator sandwiches.

Energy Boost:	✪ ✪ ✪ ✪	
Nutrients:	Vitamins C & E; folate,	
	pantothenic acid; calcium, iron,	
	magnesium; essential fatty acids	
Body Benefits:	Circulatory and nervous	
	systems; anti-stress	

Sunflower pâté
with tropicana salad

Serves 4

Sunflower pâté

3¹/₂ oz / 100 g sunflower seeds
1 tablespoon soya sauce
2 tablespoons extra virgin olive oil
1 shallot, finely chopped
7 oz / 200 g cooked green lentils
1-2 tablespoons lemon juice
1 teaspoon ground coriander
¹/₂ teaspoon black pepper
Salt to taste

1. "Toast" the sunflower seeds in a dry frying pan.
2. When they begin to pop and brown, turn off heat and add the soya sauce.
3. Stir well, then put in a mortar or food processor and grind to a coarse powder.
4. Put the oil in the frying pan, add the chopped shallot and soften for a few minutes over a low heat.
5. Put the ground sunflower seeds and cooked shallot in a food processor with the other ingredients and blend to a smooth consistency.
6. Serve with fresh French bread and tropicana salad.

Tropicana salad

4 slices fresh pineapple, peeled and diced
1 papaya, peeled and diced
¹/₂ green pepper, finely chopped
1 banana, finely chopped
1 handful raisins
2 tablespoons freshly grated (or dessicated) coconut
1 teaspoon fresh ginger, grated
4 crisp Iceberg lettuce leaves
4 litchis (lychees), peeled, stoned and halved
   to garnish (optional)

Tropicana dressing

7 fl oz / 200 ml coconut milk
¹/₂ teaspoon curry powder
1 teaspoon mustard
2 teaspoons lemon juice
2 teaspoons maple syrup
Pinch of sea salt

1. Mix the pineapple, papaya, green pepper, banana, raisins, coconut and grated ginger in a bowl.
2. Place an equal amount on each lettuce leaf.
3. Arrange the leaves on a serving plate.
4. Mix all the tropicana dressing ingredients and add a teaspoonful to each leaf. Garnish with litchis.

Energy Boost:	✪ ✪ ✪ ✪
Nutrients:	Vitamins C & E; niacin; iron, zinc, magnesium, calcium, manganese
Body Benefits:	Immune, circulatory, nervous and urino-genital systems; bones

Spicy chickpeas

Serves 4

2 tablespoons extra virgin olive oil
1 teaspoon ground cumin
1 teaspoon ground coriander seeds
2 cloves garlic, finely chopped
1 onion, chopped
1 lb / 450 g cooked chickpeas
6 tomatoes, skinned and chopped
2 tablespoons fresh parsley, finely chopped
1 teaspoon dried thyme
Pinch of chilli pepper
1 teaspoon fresh, grated ginger
3$\frac{1}{2}$ fl oz / 100 ml water or vegetable stock
Sea salt and pepper

1. Heat the oil gently in a large saucepan or wok.
2. Add the cumin, coriander, garlic and onion.
3. Stir-fry for 3–4 minutes, add the chickpeas, and then the rest of the ingredients.
4. Bring to the boil and simmer gently for 15 minutes, adding a little water from time to time if necessary.
5. Adjust seasoning and serve with lightly steamed, fresh, green beans, and basmati rice cooked with red lentils (known as khichuri).

POWER LUNCHES

Energy Boost:	✪ ✪ ✪ ✪ ✪
Nutrients:	Vitamins C & E, B-group; iron, calcium, magnesium, zinc
Body Benefit:	Whole body

Potato and broccoli
with watercress salad

Serves 4

Potato and broccoli
1³/₄ lbs / 800 g potatoes, quartered
9 oz / 250 g broccoli, cut into small florets
Chives, finely chopped

Tahini dressing
3 tablespoons tahini
3 tablespoons lemon juice
3 tablespoons cold water
1 clove garlic, crushed
¹/₂ teaspoon salt

1. Boil the potatoes in lightly salted water and cool under cold running water.
2. Steam the broccoli until tender and cool under cold running water.
3. Put the potatoes and broccoli into a serving bowl.
4. Combine the ingredients for the tahini dressing and mix gently with the vegetables.
5. Garnish with chives.

Watercress salad
1 tablespoon sesame seeds
2 bunches watercress, coarsely chopped
   (discard the thick ends of the stalks)
4 sticks celery, finely chopped
8 radishes, sliced

1. "Toast" the sesame seeds in a dry frying pan.
2. Place the watercress in a salad bowl with the celery and radishes on top.
3. Garnish with the toasted sesame seeds.

Energy Boost:	✪ ✪ ✪
Nutrients:	Vitamins C, B6, pantothenic acid, folate; iron, calcium, zinc
Body Benefits:	Immune and nervous systems; detoxifying, anti-stress

sustaining **dinners**

energy loading through the night

Ratatouille
with polenta cakes

Serves 4

Ratatouille

2 onions, sliced
5 tablespoons extra virgin olive oil
2 small eggplants (aubergines), chopped
2 small zucchini (courgettes), sliced
1 red pepper, sliced
1 green pepper, sliced
2 cloves of garlic, crushed
1 lb / 450 g ripe tomatoes, skinned
  and chopped
1 small bunch fresh basil, chopped
  (but keep some leaves whole for garnish)
Water
Sea salt and pepper
Tomato paste

1. Sauté the onions in the olive oil and add the other vegetables one at a time in the order given above.
2. Stir in the basil (keeping a few leaves to garnish the dish) and cook for two more minutes, adding extra water if required.
3. Season with salt and pepper, turn down the heat, cover and simmer gently for approximately 20 minutes.
4. Remove the lid and simmer for a further 5 minutes, thickening with a little tomato paste. Garnish with fresh basil.

Polenta cakes

Makes 12 cakes

11 oz / 300 g pre-cooked polenta
2 teaspoons herbes de Provence
$1/2$ teaspoon sea salt
Pinch of black pepper
10 fl oz / 275 ml boiling water
Grapeseed oil

1. Put the polenta in a bowl, add the herbs, salt, pepper and mix well.
2. Gradually pour in the boiling water and stir to form a thick dough. Leave for 5 minutes, then knead to an even consistency.
4. Break off handfuls of the dough and mould them into small round cakes, 2 in (5 cm) in diameter by $1/2$ in (1.5 cm) thick.
5. Shallow-fry the cakes in a little oil until golden brown, turning frequently.
6. Serve with the ratatouille and thick slices of fresh, country bread.

Energy Boost:	✪ ✪ ✪ ✪ ✪
Nutrients:	Vitamins A, C and E, B-group; calcium, magnesium, iron, zinc, selenium; essential fatty acids
Body Benefits:	Immune and digestive systems

Carrot and almond jacket potatoes
with herb salad

Serves 4

Carrot and almond jacket potatoes
4 large baking potatoes
2 tablespoons extra virgin olive oil
4 large carrots, julienned
2¹/₂ oz / 75 g almonds, chopped
1 teaspoon orange zest
1 teaspoon maple syrup
Sea salt and pepper to taste

1. Wash and dry the potatoes and rub in a little olive oil.
2. Pierce them a few times with a fork and bake in a pre-heated oven at 400°F, 200°C (Gas Mark 6) for approximately 75 minutes or until flesh is soft.
3. Put the rest of the olive oil in a frying pan, add the julienned carrots and sauté gently for a few minutes.
4. Add the almonds and cook for another 2 minutes.
5. Add the orange zest, maple syrup, salt and pepper to taste.
6. Turn the heat down as low as possible and simmer until the carrots soften.
7. When the potatoes are cooked, remove them from the oven and cut a deep cross in the top of each one.
8. Gently open out the potatoes by pressing on the four slits of the cross, sprinkle a little sea salt onto the flesh and add some of the carrot and almond mixture.
9. Serve with herb salad and tarragon dressing.

Herb salad
1 small head of red lettuce, shredded
6-8 sorrel leaves, chopped
Handful of beetroot leaves, chopped
Bunch of coriander leaves, chopped
6-8 dandelion leaves (or chicory), chopped

Mix all the ingredients together in a salad bowl and serve with tarragon dressing.

Tarragon dressing
3 tablespoons lemon juice
1 stalk fresh tarragon
¹/₄ teaspoon salt
1 clove garlic
3¹/₂ fl oz / 100 ml safflower oil
Extra virgin olive oil to taste
Pinch of pepper

Put all the ingredients (except for the olive oil) in a blender and whizz for 30 seconds. Add the olive oil to taste.

Energy Boost:	✪ ✪ ✪
Nutrients:	Vitamins C & E; calcium, iron; essential fatty acids
Body Benefits:	Heart; circulatory system

Aloo gobi

Serves 4

2 tablespoons extra virgin olive oil
Pinch of asafoetida
1 teaspoon turmeric
$1/2$ teaspoon cayenne pepper
1 teaspoon ground cumin
3 tomatoes, peeled and chopped
1 tablespoon maple syrup
$1/2$ teaspoon sea salt
9 fl oz / 250 ml water
1 lb / 450 g potatoes, quartered
1 medium cauliflower, separated into florets
1 teaspoon garam masala

1. Heat the oil in a large, heavy casserole, wok or karai, add
the asafoetida, turmeric, cayenne and cumin and sauté for
a few seconds.
2. Add the tomatoes, maple syrup and salt and cook for a
further minute.
3. Pour in the water, bring to the boil and add the potatoes,
then cover and simmer for 10 minutes.
4. Add the cauliflower, bring back to the boil and simmer for
a further 5 minutes (or until the vegetables are tender).
5. Sprinkle with garam masala and serve with basmati rice
cooked in coconut milk with cumin and lime juice.

Energy Boost:	✪ ✪ ✪ ✪ ✪
Nutrients:	Vitamins C & E; niacin, vitamin B6, folate; iron
Body Benefits:	Immune and circulatory systems; skin

Vegetable crumble

Serves 4

7 oz / 200 g flour
2 tablespoons flaked almonds
$4^{1}/_{2}$ oz / 125 g vegetable margarine
1 onion, sliced
2 medium carrots, sliced
2 sticks celery, sliced
$1/4$ cabbage, shredded
$4^{1}/_{2}$ oz / 125 g hazel nuts, chopped
1 tablespoon yeast extract dissolved in 6 fl oz (175 ml)
    boiling water
8 oz / 225 g tomatoes, skinned and chopped
Sea salt and pepper to taste; flaked almonds to garnish

1. For the crumble, blend the flour with the almonds and half
the margarine, keeping a tablespoon of flour aside.
2. Melt the rest of the margarine in a large pan and gently
sauté the onions, carrots, celery and cabbage until soft. Add
the hazelnuts and heat through. Stir in the remaining flour.
3. Pour in the yeast extract mixture. Stir until it thickens.
4. Add the tomatoes, season with salt and pepper, and pour
into a greased casserole dish.
5. Sprinkle the crumble mixture on top, garnish with flaked
almonds and cook in the oven for approximately one hour
at 350°F, 180°C (Gas Mark 4) until golden brown.
6. Serve with steamed French beans and sweetcorn.

Energy Boost:	✪ ✪ ✪ ✪ ✪
Nutrients:	B-group vitamins; calcium, iron
Body Benefits:	Immune and circulatory systems; bones, soft tissue; anti-stress

Asparagus, bean curd and mushrooms

Serves 4

2 tablespoons extra virgin olive oil
8 oz / 225 g bean curd (tofu), diced
1 small leek, sliced
8 oz / 225 g oyster mushrooms, cleaned and whole
1 clove garlic, crushed
1 teaspoon fresh ginger, finely chopped
1 bunch green asparagus, cut into small pieces
  (discard the bottom 2 in / 5 cm of the stalks)
$3^1/_2$ fl oz / 100 ml vegetable stock or water
2 tablespoons soya sauce; 2 tablespoons dry sherry
1 teaspoon cornflour, dissolved in a little warm water

1. Heat the oil in a wok or large frying pan and stir-fry the bean curd for a couple of minutes.
2. Add the leek and stir for another minute, then the mushrooms, garlic and ginger, stir-frying until the mushrooms release their moisture.
3. Add the asparagus, stock, soya sauce and sherry, then cover and simmer very gently until the asparagus is tender.
4. Add the cornflour and stir until the sauce thickens.
5. Serve with noodles.

Energy Boost:	✪ ✪ ✪ ✪
Nutrients:	Niacin, folate, biotin; calcium, iron, zinc, magnesium
Body Benefits:	Immune, circulatory and nervous systems; skin and hair; bones and soft tissues

Spinach parcels
with onion sauce

Serves 4

Spinach parcels

1 lb / 450 g fresh spinach

2 tablespoons olive oil

8 oz / 225 g bean curd (tofu), diced

4 small scallions (spring onions), finely chopped

1 clove garlic, finely chopped

1 tablespoon soya sauce

$1/2$ teaspoon crushed coriander seeds

$1/2$ teaspoon crushed cumin seeds

Sea salt and pepper to taste

1 packet strudel dough sheets

1. Wash the spinach and place, wet, in a large saucepan over a moderate heat, without adding further water. The spinach will steam in the water left on the leaves after rinsing.

2. When the leaves soften, remove them from the pan with a slotted spoon and chop them.

3. Heat the oil in a frying pan and sauté the bean curd for 2–3 minutes. Add the scallions and the garlic, then the soya sauce, and cook for a minute before adding the spinach, coriander and cumin.

4. Heat through and add sea salt and pepper to taste, then remove from heat.

5. Open out a sheet of strudel dough, brush with olive oil and place two generous spoonfuls of the spinach filling in the middle of the sheet.

6. Fold sheet into a parcel and repeat steps 6-7 until you have used up all the filling, then brush each parcel with oil.

7. Bake at 425°F, 220°C (Gas Mark 7) until golden.

8. Serve with onion sauce, new potatoes, peas and carrots.

Onion sauce

2 tablespoons olive oil

8 oz / 225 g onions, finely chopped

2 tablespoons soya sauce

2 tablespoons wheat flour

14 fl oz / 400 ml vegetable stock

$3^1/2$ oz / 100 ml soya milk

Sea salt and pepper to taste

1. Heat the oil gently in a casserole.

2. Add the onions and soften without allowing to brown.

3. Put in the soya sauce and wheat flour; stir well.

4. Gradually pour in the stock, stirring continuously, then simmer for a few minutes.

5. Add the soya milk, still stirring, and heat through.

6. Season with salt and pepper, and serve.

Energy Boost:	✪ ✪ ✪ ✪
Nutrients:	Vitamin C; niacin, folate, pantothenic acid; calcium, iron
Body Benefits:	Nervous system; anti–stress

Sweet potato and hiziki

Serves 4

1 cup dried hiziki (seaweed)
4 tablespoons extra virgin olive oil
1 lb / 450 g sweet potatoes, peeled
    and cut into thin sticks
3¹/₂ oz / 100 ml vegetable stock
¹/₂ teaspoon sea salt
1 tablespoon maple syrup
1 tablespoon dry sherry
1 tablespoon soya sauce
1 tablespoon tahini
Gomasio to garnish

1. Rinse the seaweed in cold water.
2. Put in a bowl and cover with hot water.
3. Leave to soak for 15-20 minutes, adding more hot water from time to time to keep the seaweed completely immersed.
4. Discard the soaking water and rinse again.
5. Heat the oil gently in a wok or big pot.
6. Add the sweet potato and stir-fry for a few minutes, then put in the seaweed and cook for a further two minutes.
7. Add the rest of the cooking ingredients and stir. Cover and simmer gently for 5 minutes.
8. Garnish with the gomasio and serve with a mixture of rice and wild rice.

Energy Boost:	✪ ✪ ✪ ✪ ✪
Nutrients:	Vitamins A & E; B-group; iron, iodine
Body Benefits:	Immune, endocrine and nervous systems; skin

Nettle and lasagne bake

Serves 4

Nettle and lasagne bake

7 oz / 200 g fresh young nettle tips – use gloves (if you have
  difficulty finding nettles, curly kale can be used instead)
1 onion, finely chopped
1 carrot, finely chopped
7 oz / 200 g mushrooms, chopped
2 sticks celery, finely sliced
2 tablespoons extra virgin olive oil
8 oz / 225 g tomatoes, peeled and chopped
1 teaspoon lemon juice
1 sprig fresh thyme, finely chopped (or $\frac{1}{2}$ teaspoon dried)
1 bay leaf
Tomato paste
Sea salt and pepper to taste
1 packet lasagne sheets ("no pre-cooking required" variety)

1. Pick and wash the nettles using gloves, then steam in a
little water until soft. Remove from the pan and chop finely.
2. Sauté the onion, carrot, mushrooms and celery in the oil,
then add the steamed nettles, tomatoes, lemon juice, herbs
and a little tomato paste.
3. Simmer for about 5 minutes, or until mixture thickens.
4. Set aside while you make the white sauce.

White sauce

1 oz / 25 g vegetable margarine
2 tablespoons wheat flour
7 fl oz / 200 ml soya milk
Pinch of freshly grated nutmeg; sea salt and pepper

1. Melt the margarine gently in a saucepan and add the flour,
stirring for a minute.
2. Add the soya milk a little at a time, stirring continuously.
3. Bring to boil and simmer for a couple of minutes.
4. Add nutmeg, salt and pepper to taste.

Lasagne topping

8 oz / 225 g bean curd (tofu)
3 tablespoons soya sauce
2 tablespoons olive oil
4 fl oz / 125 ml water
2 teaspoons mustard
Salt and pepper

Blend all the ingredients to a smooth paste.

To make up the dish

Grease an ovenproof dish and cover the bottom with a thin
layer of white sauce. Put a layer of pasta on top, then add
a layer of nettle filling. Continue layering in this sequence,
ending with a layer of pasta. Spread the topping over the
bake. Transfer to a hot oven (425°F / 220°C / Gas Mark 7)
and bake for approximately 25 minutes (or until the lasagne
is soft). Serve with chopped cucumber and mint, dressed in
lemon juice.

Energy Boost:	✪ ✪ ✪ ✪ ✪	
Nutrients :	Vitamins A & C, niacin, folate, pantothenic acid, calcium and iron	
Body Benefits:	Immune and circulatory systems, bones, soft tissues; anti-stress	

Stuffed mushrooms
with spiced peaches

Serves 4

Stuffed mushrooms

12-16 large, flat mushrooms
3 tablespoons extra virgin olive oil
2 cloves garlic, finely chopped
1 shallot, finely chopped
1 sprig fresh (or $1/2$ teaspoon dried) rosemary, chopped
1 tablespoon soya sauce
4-5 tablespoons breadcrumbs
1 small bunch parsley, finely chopped

1. Remove the mushroom stalks and set them aside.
2. Scoop out the black gills inside the mushroom caps with a teaspoon and discard.
3. Place the caps upside down (edges upward) in an oiled oven-proof dish or baking tray.
4. Finely chop the mushroom stalks and sauté in olive oil for one minute.
5. Add the garlic and shallot, and heat through.
6. Put in the rosemary and soya sauce and simmer until the mushrooms release their moisture.
7. Add enough breadcrumbs to soak up the liquid, then remove from the heat and add the parsley.
8. Fill the mushroom caps with the mixture.
9. Bake for 5-10 minutes at 400°F, 200°C (Gas Mark 6) until golden brown.
10. Serve with spiced peaches and steamed new potatoes.

Spiced peaches

4 big, ripe peaches, peeled, stoned and sliced
4 tablespoons maple syrup
2 tablespoons lemon juice
2 teaspoons ground, roasted cumin
$1/4$ teaspoon cayenne pepper
$1/2$ teaspoon sea salt
Black pepper to taste

1. Put the peaches in a serving bowl.
2. Mix the other ingredients together, except the black pepper, and pour over the peaches.
3. Sprinkle with black pepper and serve immediately.

Energy Boost:	✪ ✪ ✪
Nutrients:	Vitamin C; folate, biotin; iron
Body Benefits:	Immune and nervous systems; skin and hair; detoxifying

Crispy lettuce rolls
with almond dressing

Makes 12 rolls

Crispy lettuce rolls
2 scallions (spring onions), finely chopped
1 avocado, peeled, stoned and diced
1 carrot, grated
1 stick celery, finely chopped
$^1/_2$ red pepper, deseeded and finely chopped

1 handful of fresh sprouts (sunflower, alfalfa or bean)
12 large lettuce leaves (a mixture of green and red)
A few edible flowers (e.g. nasturtium, marigold or borage), or some sprigs of fresh herbs (e.g. basil, parsley or coriander)

1. Combine the scallions, avocado, carrot, celery, red pepper and sprouts in a bowl, and mix well.
2. Place a tablespoon of the mixture in the middle of a lettuce leaf and add a spoonful of almond dressing.
3. Fold the two sides of the leaf into the middle, then roll it up from stalk to tip, and fasten with a cocktail stick.
4. Repeat with the other leaves.
5. Serve garnished with edible flowers or herb sprigs.

Almond dressing
4 tablespoons almond butter
4 tablespoons lemon juice
4 tablespoons water
Sea salt and pepper to taste

1. Stir together almond butter, lemon juice and water.
2. Season with salt and black pepper.

For variety, try the following variation:
6 tablespoons extra virgin olive oil
1 clove garlic, crushed
2 tablespoons almond butter
4 or 5 fresh tarragon leaves, finely chopped
   (or $\frac{1}{2}$ teaspoon dried)
4 tablespoons lemon juice; sea salt and pepper to taste

1. Place all ingredients in a bowl and mix well.
2. Season with salt and black pepper.

Energy Boost:	✪ ✪ ✪ ✪ ✪	
Nutrients:	Vitamins A, C, & E, B-group; iron, calcium, magnesium, zinc; essential fatty acids	
Body Benefits:	Nervous, circulatory and immune systems; anti-stress	

Greek olive and lime pâté

15 Greek olives, stoned and finely chopped
$3\frac{1}{2}$ oz / 100 g cooked butter beans
Juice of $\frac{1}{2}$ lime
1 tablespoon extra virgin olive oil
Small pinch of cayenne pepper
Sea salt and pepper to taste
Slices of lime and radish to garnish

1. Combine all the ingredients in a mixing bowl and mash to a smooth consistency.
2. Transfer to serving dish and garnish with thin slices of lime and crisp red radish.
3. Serve with rough oatcakes or melba toast.

Energy Boost:	✪ ✪ ✪ ✪	
Nutrients:	Vitamins C & E; niacin, folate, pantothenic acid; calcium, magnesium, iron, zinc; essential fatty acids	
Body Benefits:	Nervous and immune systems; bones; anti-stress	

Pistachio and raisin halwa

1 cup toasted sesame seeds
2 tablespoons raw sugar
2 tablespoons unsalted pistachio nuts, finely chopped
1 tablespoon sun-dried raisins
2 tablespoons honey

Energy Boost:	✪ ✪ ✪ ✪
Nutrients:	Vitamin E; niacin, biotin, pantothenic acid; selenium, calcium, magnesium, iron, zinc
Body Benefits:	Immune, nervous and endocrine systems; skin and hair; anti-stress

1. Toast the sesame seeds in a dry pan, allow to cool, then grind with the sugar in a mortar to a powder.
2. Put in a bowl, add the rest of the ingredients and knead to form a stiff dough.
3. Shape the dough into a rectangular loaf.
4. Refrigerate for half an hour before slicing and serving.

For variety, try using other nuts in place of pistachios.

Mint and raisin spread

9 oz / 250 g raisins
A handful of fresh mint leaves
Hot water

Energy Boost:	✪ ✪ ✪
Nutrients:	Vitamin C; niacin, biotin, pantothenic acid; iron
Body Benefits:	Immune, circulatory, and digestive systems; skin and hair; anti-stress

1. Put the raisins and the mint in a blender, adding a little hot water at a time until the mixture blends to form a smooth paste.
2. Serve spread on freshly toasted, wholemeal muffins.

Ruby reviver

Makes 1 serving

1 tomato
1 stick celery
$1/4$ lemon, peeled
$1/4$ cucumber, peeled
$1/2$ beetroot, peeled
2 carrots
1-2 sprigs of fresh lovage (or basil, chives or parsley)
Sea salt and black pepper to taste
1-2 drops Tabasco sauce (optional)
Slice of lemon to garnish

1. Cut the ingredients into chunks and press them through the juicer, one at a time.
2. Add sea salt and black pepper to taste and pour into a tall glass with one or two drops of Tabasco sauce.
3. Decorate glass with a slice of lemon and drink through a thick straw.

Energy Boost:	✪ ✪ ✪
Nutrients:	Vitamins A & C; folate, pantothenic acid; all minerals
Body Benefits:	Nervous and immune systems; detoxifying

Strawberry and banana smoothie

Makes 1 serving

5 fl oz / 150 ml thick apple juice
8 fresh strawberries, stalks removed
1 banana, peeled
Sprig of fresh mint

Energy Boost:	✪ ✪ ✪
Nutrients:	Vitamin C
Body Benefits:	Immune systems

Put the apple juice, strawberries and banana in a blender and whizz for 30 seconds. Serve in a tall glass, garnished with fresh mint.

Index

Acknowledgments

Nic Rowley and Kirsten Hartvig
would like to thank Anna Mews,
Françoise Nassivet, Jackie Young,
Jill Byrne, Joyce Thomas, Lilly Jensen,
Katinka Thielemans, Liz Pearson,
Susie Mitchison and Judy Dean
for their help and inspiration.
The authors' website is at
www.labergerie.net.

The publishers would like
to thank retail outlets David Mellors
and Divertimenti for the loan of
props used in this book.